Write It Right

Writing a Journal

By Cecilia Minden and Kate Roth

Published in the United States of America by
Cherry Lake Publishing
Ann Arbor, Michigan
www.cherrylakepublishing.com

Reading Adviser: Marla Conn MS, Ed., Literacy specialist, Read-Ability, Inc.
Book Designer: Felicia Macheske
Character Illustrator: Carol Herring

Photo Credits: © Monkey Business Images/Shutterstock, 5; © MaLija/Shutterstock, 7; © diignat/Shutterstock, 9; © Rob Hainer/ Shutterstock, 11; © Zurijeta/Shutterstock, 21

Graphics Throughout: © simple surface/Shutterstock.com; © Mix3r/Shutterstock.com; © Artefficient/Shutterstock.com; © lemony/ Shutterstock.com; © Svetolk/Shutterstock.com; © EV-DA/Shutterstock.com; © briddy/Shutterstock.com; © IreneArt/Shutterstock.com

Library of Congress Cataloging-in-Publication Data

Names: Minden, Cecilia, author. | Roth, Kate, author. | Herring, Carol, illustrator.
Title: Writing a journal / by Cecilia Minden and Kate Roth ; illustrated by Carol Herring.
Description: Ann Arbor : Cherry Lake Publishing, [2019] | Series: Write it
 right | Audience: K to grade 3. | Includes bibliographical references and index.
Identifiers: LCCN 2019006003| ISBN 9781534147171 (hardcover) | ISBN
 9781534150034 (pbk.) | ISBN 9781534148604 (PDF) | ISBN 9781534151468
 (hosted ebook)
Subjects: LCSH: Diaries—Authorship—Juvenile literature.
Classification: LCC PN4390 .M57 2019 | DDC 808/.06692—dc23
LC record available at https://lccn.loc.gov/2019006003

Cherry Lake Publishing would like to acknowledge the work of The Partnership for 21st Century Skills.
Please visit *www.p21.org* for more information.

Printed in the United States of America
Corporate Graphics

Table of
CONTENTS

CHAPTER ONE

All About You

A **journal** is a written collection of your feelings and thoughts. It is a place where you can record your **opinions**. You can also write about events. What you write about is up to you!

You can keep a journal in different ways. Some people type their journals using computers. Others handwrite in notebooks.

Here's what you'll need to complete the activities in this book:

- Notebook
- Pen

A journal can go with you wherever you go.

Create a decorative cover for your journal.

CHAPTER TWO

Write About a Place

What do writers do when they need an idea to write about? Many of them write about what they know.

For your first journal **entry**, write about a place. Start by thinking about a place you know well. Close your eyes. Picture that place in your head. Now describe the place in your journal. You can also write about why it is important to you.

How else can you come up with a journal idea?

Think of a place that makes you happy.

ACTIVITY

I Like to Go to ...

INSTRUCTIONS:

1. Make a list of places you like to visit.

2. Choose one to write about.

3. In your journal, describe the place. Imagine you are writing for someone who has never been there. Use a lot of **details** to share your **information**.

4. Explain what you like about that place. How do you feel when you are there?

ICING

8

1. The lake
2. The movies
3. Grandma's kitchen ✓

August 24, 2019

One of my favorite places is my grandma's kitchen. Grandma's kitchen always smells terrific. It smells like cinnamon and spice. There are tall windows that let in lots of light. Grandma has a big wooden table where we mix up cookies. I like to roll them and cut them out. They are baked and cooled. Then we ice them in bright colors and cover with sprinkles.

CHAPTER THREE

Write About an Event

Do you need another idea? Write about an event. An event is something that happens. Events are usually special in some way.

Use your senses to describe the event. What did you see? What did you hear? What could you smell? Did you feel happy or scared? Make a short list before you write the journal entry. Put the actions of the event in the order in which they happened. This is called **chronological** order.

Do you like to go to amusement parks?

Think of a place where you had a great time.

What Happened?

INSTRUCTIONS:

1. Think of events that happened to you.
2. Choose one to write about.
3. Try to remember everything that happened.
4. List what happened in chronological order.
5. Use the list to help you write your journal entry.

Sample Events

- My little sister was born.
- I broke my leg in third grade.
- Taylor and I went to Spring Lake Amusement Park ✓
    1. He wanted to ride the roller coaster.
    2. I had never been on a roller coaster.
    3. Taylor said it was fun, so I gave it a try.
    4. I loved it!

April 23, 2019

I went to the Spring Lake Amusement Park with my best friend and his family. It was a perfect day, with blue skies and white clouds.

Taylor wanted to go on the roller coaster. I'd never been on a roller coaster. It was very tall, and the cars were going really fast. Taylor told me it was fun to be up high and go fast. He encouraged me to give it a try.

Finally, I decided to go for it. It was scary at first, but then it was fun. Taylor and I screamed long and loud. I loved it. I didn't want to get off!

CHAPTER FOUR

Write About Your Feelings

A journal is just for you. Writing can help you think about feelings. What makes you sad? What makes you happy? Writing can help you understand your feelings.

Have You Ever Felt . . .

INSTRUCTIONS:

1. Choose a feeling.
2. Think about things that make you feel that way.
3. Write about the feeling you chose in your journal.

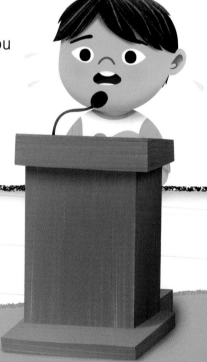

- Being happy
- Being scared ✓
- Being hungry

Things that make me feel scared:
1. Giving a speech ✓
2. Horror movies
3. Lightning

June 23, 2019

I am frightened of getting up in front of people to talk. My mouth gets dry, my hands shake, and I forget what I'm going to say. My dad told me he used to feel the same way. Now he takes a note card with him. On the card are the important points he wants to remember. He practices his speech many times until he knows it very well. He also told me to look at the back wall until I am comfortable looking at faces. Next time I have to give a speech, I am going to do all of these things.

CHAPTER FIVE

Write About Your Opinion

A journal is a great place to write your opinions. You can write about why you like or do not like something. Maybe you are not sure how you feel. That's okay. Try putting both sides of the story on paper. This can help you sort out your thoughts.

ACTIVITY

What Do You Think?

INSTRUCTIONS:

1. Make a list of things you do not like.
2. Choose one to write about.
3. Write about what you don't like in your journal.
4. Be sure to explain your opinion.

Things I Don't Like:
1. Being late
2. Cereal with milk ✓
3. Camping in the rain

November 27, 2019

I like cereal. I eat it dry as a snack. I like milk. I drink it from a glass. I do not like to pour milk on my cereal. No matter how fast I eat, the cereal gets soggy. Then the milk turns the color of the cereal. I end up with a bowl of mushy food and tinted milk. And I haven't even finished breakfast. No thanks!

CHAPTER SIX

Write About Your Wishes and Dreams

Do you have any wishes or dreams? Do you ever wish you could do something special? What do you dream of doing when you get older? Write about these wishes and dreams in your journal.

ACTIVITY

What Did You Wish For?

INSTRUCTIONS:

1. Make a list of your wishes or dreams.
2. Choose one to write about.
3. Write about it in your journal.

Things I'm Wishing For:
1. My own phone ✓
2. A gerbil
3. A trophy at the track meet

October 8, 2019

I wish I had my own phone. Mom and Dad told me I could get one on my next birthday. My birthday is 6 months away! Most of my friends have their own phone. They tease me because I don't have one. I asked my parents if I could get one earlier. They sat down with me to talk about it. They explained the cost and the responsibility that comes with having your own phone. I now understand why they are asking me to wait. But I sure wish my birthday would hurry up!

CHAPTER SEVEN

Keep Writing!

You are a special person with many things to say. Journals are books full of thoughts and feelings. Keep writing! Keep your journals in a safe place. You may want to read them again years from now. How might you change as you get older? Will you have the same interests or the same worries? It will be fun to look back on your life as a kid!

What do you think will surprise you when you read your journal in 10 years?

Ask your friends what thoughts they put in their journals.

GLOSSARY

chronological (kron-uh-LOJ-uh-kuhl) arranged in the order in which things happened

details (DEE-taylz) separate bits of information about something

entry (EN-tree) a piece of information in a journal

information (in-fur-MAY-shuhn) knowledge and facts

journal (JUR-nuhl) a record of one's thoughts and ideas

opinions (uh-PIN-yuhnz) a person's beliefs and ideas about somebody or something

For More
INFORMATION

BOOKS

Becker, Suzy. *Kids Make It Better: A Write-In, Draw-In Journal.*
New York, NY: Workman Publishing Company, 2010.

Loewen, Nancy. *It's All About You: Writing Your Own Journal.*
Minneapolis, MN: Picture Window Books, 2009.

WEBSITES

Kids Craft: Make Your Own Journal
https://www.thecountrychiccottage.net/kids-craft-make-your-own-journal
Look here for instructions and a downloadable journal kit to print.

KidsHealth—What to Do if You Can't Sleep
kidshealth.org/kid/stay_healthy/body/cant_sleep.html
Find out how writing in a journal can help you get to sleep.

INDEX

About the AUTHORS

Cecilia Minden is the former director of the Language and Literacy Program at Harvard Graduate School of Education. She earned her doctorate from the University of Virginia. Her research focused on early literacy skills and developing phonics curriculums. She is currently a literacy consultant and the author of over 100 books for children. Dr. Minden lives with her family in McKinney, Texas.

Kate Roth has a doctorate from Harvard University in language and literacy and a master's degree from Columbia University Teachers College in curriculum and teaching. Her work focuses on writing instruction in the primary grades. She has taught kindergarten, first grade, and Reading Recovery. She has also instructed hundreds of teachers from around the world in early literacy practices. She lived with her husband and three children in China for many years, and now they live in Connecticut.